SUPERSTARS OF POKER
TEXAS HOLD'EM

Antonio
"The Magician"
Esfandiari

SUPERSTARS OF POKER
TEXAS HOLD'EM

Doyle "Texas Dolly" Brunson

Johnny "Oriental Express" Chan

Antonio "The Magician" Esfandiari

Chris "Jesus" Ferguson

Gus "The Great Dane" Hansen

Jennifer Harman

Phil "The Poker Brat" Hellmuth

Phil "Tiger Woods of Poker" Ivey

Phil "Unabomber" Laak

Howard "The Professor" Lederer

Chris Moneymaker

Daniel "Kid Poker" Negreanu

Greg "Fossilman" Raymer

Texas Hold'em: The Learning Curve of Life

Antonio "The Magician" Esfandiari

Jackie Allyson

Mason Crest Publishers

Antonio "The Magician" Esfandiari

Produced by 21st Century Publishing and Communications, Inc.
Editorial by Harding House Publishing Services, Inc.

MASON CREST PUBLISHERS INC.
370 Reed Road
Broomall, Pennsylvania 19008
(866) MCP-BOOK (toll free)
www.masoncrest.com

Printed in the United States.

First Printing

9 8 7 6 5 4 3 2 1

Library of Congress Cataloging-in-Publication Data

Allyson, Jackie.
    Antonio "the Magician" Esfandiari / by Jackie Allyson.
      p. cm.—(Superstars of poker)
    Includes bibliographical references and index.
    Hardback edition: ISBN-13: 978-1-4222-0217-3
    Paperback edition: ISBN-13: 978-1-4222-0370-5
  1. Esfandiari, Antonio. 2. Poker players—Biography—Juvenile literature. 3. Poker—
Juvenile literature. I. Title.
GV1250.2.E83A44 2008
795.412092—dc22
[B]   2007012153

Publisher's notes:
All quotations in this book come from original sources, and contain the
spelling and grammatical inconsistencies of the original text.

The Web sites mentioned in this book were active at the time of publication.
The publisher is not responsible for Web sites that have changed their addresses
or discontinued operation since the date of publication. The publisher will
review and update the Web site addresses each time the book is reprinted.

CONTENTS

INTRODUCTION

by the North American Poker Council

FOR GOOD OR ILL, TEENS LOVE POKER. IT'S BECOME the Friday-night activity of choice for many adolescents. Some adults are pleased, some definitely aren't. So what's the reality?

Well, here are some facts:

- Poker keeps teens occupied in someone's living room or kitchen, rather than out drinking and cruising.

- Poker teaches young adults to pick up on social cues. As they learn to understand "tells," they're gaining insights that help them in a variety of situations.

- Poker develops the portions of the brain that deal with mathematical skills. In today's world where math and the sciences are important to many career paths, those skills are vital.

- Poker helps young adults learn self-control. Kids who have tantrums when things don't go their way don't last long in poker games. Learning to wear a "poker face" helps teens control their up-and-down emotions so they can excel in academic, social, and professional situations.

- Poker gives kids a better understanding of their own mental states. You can't learn self-control without realizing what it is you're controlling. Poker helps adolescents recognize their feelings, which in turn, allows them to get a handle on their emotions.

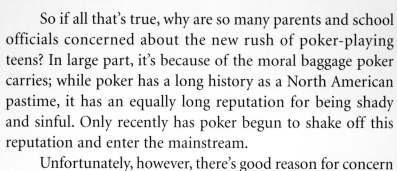

So if all that's true, why are so many parents and school officials concerned about the new rush of poker-playing teens? In large part, it's because of the moral baggage poker carries; while poker has a long history as a North American pastime, it has an equally long reputation for being shady and sinful. Only recently has poker begun to shake off this reputation and enter the mainstream.

Unfortunately, however, there's good reason for concern when it comes to teens and poker. Here's why: teens who play poker face a real risk of gambling addiction.

So should parents and educators shout a loud, resounding "NO!" when it comes to young adults and poker? Well, that seldom works when it comes to teens; poker is out there, and it's being heavily marketed to the younger generation. A far better choice is to take a look at the realities and assist young adults in developing the skills they'll need to handle poker's challenges wisely.

That's what this series does. It allows teens to learn from the best: the superstars who win time after time. These stars have important life lessons to offer teenagers, and their message is clear: you're not going to have the mental capacity to win if you drink, use drugs, don't get enough sleep, don't eat healthy, or if you allow poker to consume your life.

And isn't that a great message for teens and adults alike to hear?

1

The Magician

◆ ◆ ◆ ◆

HE HELD UP HIS CARDS IN TRIUMPH AND SHOWED THEM to the crowd. Two aces. He may as well have been holding $1.4 million dollars—that's how much he earned when those pocket aces clinched the championship win. He is Antonio Esfandiari, but in the poker world, they call him "The Magician."

Poker's New Star

Until that dramatic day, Antonio had never placed better than third in a major poker tournament, and most of his finishes were lower and farther from the big money. At the World Poker Tour (WPT) 2004 L.A. Poker Classic, Antonio's luck finally changed. That's where he beat Vinnie Vinh

You can call him Antonio, Amir, "The Magician," or even champ. Although Antonio Esfandiari is a relative newcomer to poker, he's made a big impression on the fans and on other poker players as well. He has a personality—and a mouth—made for the age of televised poker tournaments.

to win the No Limit Hold'em championship. The prize was nearly $1.4 million—the biggest the WPT had awarded to that date.

Television cameras captured the game—a game in which Antonio conquered a field of 382 players—and broadcast his victory all over the world. It was the first time such a young player had won a televised tournament—or a million-dollar prize—and youthful television viewers immediately connected with Antonio. Attractive, young, stylish, and self-assured, Antonio was televised poker's newest star.

Not everyone in the poker world, however, was as taken with Antonio as his new television fans were. Many poker players, with decades more experience and millions more in wins, saw the young magician as arrogant, **egotistical**, and boastful. He made jokes, tossed around insults, and taunted other players at the table, then celebrated gleefully when he won. It was the poker equivalent to a wide receiver running in a huge touchdown and then spiking the ball in the linebacker's face—the fans in the stands might love it, but it's poor sportsmanship and disrespectful to the other team.

The other players may have found Antonio obnoxious, but that didn't change a simple fact—he was talented. Very talented. Some people would try to chalk up Antonio's success to beginner's luck. They wouldn't be able to write off Antonio for long. Just two months after his big WPT victory, Antonio had another huge win that he'd be able to brag about for the rest of his life. It came at the 2004 World Series of Poker (WSOP), the biggest and most respected poker tournament on earth.

The Biggest Tournament on Earth

The first WSOP was played in 1970 by seven of the best poker players in the world. Those first World Series legends were Johnny Moss, "Amarillo Slim" Preston, "Sailor" Roberts, Walter "Puggy" Pearson, Crandall Addington, Carl Cannon, and Doyle "Texas Dolly" Brunson. Since then, the World Series has grown every year.

Today, the tournament consists of preliminary events followed by the main event: the $10,000 No Limit Hold'em World Championship. In addition to the prize money, event winners receive bracelets as signs of their achievement. For many people, those coveted bracelets are the ultimate sign of success in the high-stakes poker world. Every

The World Series of Poker championship has grown enormously from its first event in 1970. At that tournament, only seven players were invited to participate, and the winner was "elected." Today, as seen in this photo from 2006, the number of players has increased. But the number of players isn't the only thing that is bigger—so is the purse.

spring, thousands of poker greats and unknown hopefuls descend on Las Vegas, Nevada. Their destination is the Rio Hotel and Casino— home of the WSOP. Their hope is to become a poker superstar, and possibly a millionaire.

In the spring of 2004, Antonio "The Magician" Esfandiari was one of those hopefuls coughing up thousands of dollars in buy-in fees for the chance at a bracelet and the respect it brings. He needed to prove to all the doubters that his WPT win was more than good luck, and on May 10, 2004, he did just that.

Proving Himself

Antonio proved he was no one-shot deal by winning the WSOP's $2000 Pot Limit Hold'em event. As a preliminary event, the $184,860 prize money was not nearly as much as his WPT championship.

Antonio is a fan favorite, especially after he began racking up WPT and WSOP wins (earning the coveted gold bracelet). He's become a celebrity in the poker world, and he's enjoying every minute of it. But he doesn't let the fame distract him from his goal of becoming the best poker player in the world.

However, by winning the event, Antonio earned something that in the poker world can be even more valuable than money: a WSOP gold bracelet.

Winning a WSOP bracelet catapulted Antonio into the realm of the poker elite. From now on, the young magician would be accepted as one of the world's best players. As a top player, he now enjoys respect and celebrity status. For Antonio, the money and success are dreams come true. But for him, perhaps the best part of all is the respect and celebrity that came with his big wins. In an interview for the *San Francisco Chronicle*, he revealed:

> **"I love being on TV. I was such a dork in high school. All I ever wanted was to be popular. My dream was for someone, someday, to ask for my autograph."**

Now Antonio's dream comes true nearly every day. Fans watch him on television, ask for advice on his Web site, and travel to see him play live in tournaments. Fans lucky enough to speak with Antonio face to face ask for his autograph, request snippets of poker wisdom, and even seek bits of fashion advice.

As a kid, Antonio could never have imagined the life that was waiting for him just a few years down the road. With a childhood scarred by war, upheaval, and loss, a life of respect and celebrity did not appear to be in the cards. But young Antonio was not the type of person who was going to sit around and wait for life to happen to him. From a very early age, he decided to seize opportunities and make his own luck. He's taken huge risks along the way, and even jeopardized his relationship with his father, to pursue his dream. But for Antonio, the risks have paid off.

Unlikely Champion
♠ ♠ ♠ ♠

ANTONIO'S STORY BEGINS FAR FROM POKER, CASINOS, Las Vegas, and all the things that define his life today. His story starts under a different name in a country with a different way of life. The unlikely poker champion's road began in a Middle Eastern country where it is illegal to even own playing cards.

A World Away

Antonio was born Amir Esfandiari on December 8, 1978, in Iran. The family was wealthy, but their wealth didn't bring security. As Esfandiari explained in an interview for *Bluff* magazine:

The Iran-born Antonio Esfandiari moved to the United States when he was only nine years old. Though his childhood in this new country was difficult, it was much less so than if his family had stayed in Iran. Antonio made the most of the opportunities found here, and he has the success to show for it.

"I remember we were at war with Iraq and there would be bombs going off and we'd have to go and hide out in the basements of the apartment that we used to live in."

Amir was nine when the family came to San Jose, California. The money they brought with them was worth very little in U.S. dollars. To make matters worse, they spoke very little English. And yet Antonio told *Bluff*:

"We were very lucky and my father gave up his entire life and everything in Iran to bring us to America and give his kids a better life."

Amir's mother, however, did not feel the same way. After only three weeks, she packed her bags and told her family she was flying to Los Angeles to visit her brother. She never came back, and the family soon learned she had returned to Iran.

Broken Home, Broken Hearts

For six months after his mother's departure, Amir cried every night when he got home from school. To make matters worse, at school he was taunted for the shape of his nose, called "towel head," and teased about his name. Trying to fit in, Amir changed his name to Anthony. His younger brother, Pasha, changed his name to Paul.

Anthony was a straight-A student, but academic success wasn't what he craved. What Anthony wanted more than anything else was his peers' respect and admiration. He thought money would be the best way to get it. He got a job, and at just eleven years old, he was making $400 per week selling newspaper subscriptions. By sixteen, he was a waiter at a popular steakhouse. He had the money to treat his friends to gifts and nights on the town. Anthony's friends were impressed.

His father was not. One night, when Anthony was just seventeen, sparks flew in another confrontation between him and his father. Anthony packed his bags and walked out the door. He didn't return.

A New Life

Anthony rented an apartment and continued working at the restaurant. One night during his shift, the bartender pulled out a deck of cards and performed a magic trick. Anthony was mesmerized, and magic became his passion. He began practicing magic twelve hours a day and performing for the tables he served at the restaurant. According to an article in *All In* magazine:

"'I love messing with people's heads,' says Esfandiari. 'Before I started doing magic, I was shy. After? Never.'"

WPT® Poker

THE OFFICIAL WORLD POKER TOUR™ MAGAZINE

CHIP POWER

Beyond tells! How to know what they've got by how much they bet

SPADES & SORCERY

Tactical tricks from Hold 'Em 'Magician' Antonio Esfandiari

FISHING FOR EASY PREY

How smart players exploit novices

Antonio became fascinated with magic at an early age. Showing the dedication he would always exhibit to conquer most things he tries, Antonio became a top-notch magician. For Antonio, it also helped him conquer a problem common to many young people—shyness. It also provided him with a poker nickname: The Magician.

Poker and other forms of gambling are forbidden in Islam, the religion of Antonio's native Iran. It is believed that gambling encourages people not to work, instead earning their money the "lazy" way. The Prophet Muhammad also noted that even losing is often no deterrent, perhaps one of the first descriptions of addiction.

Soon Anthony discovered another talent. One night he tagged along with his roommate to a poker tournament at a local card room. Anthony watched the action and played a few side games. A couple weeks later, he entered a small tournament at the Garden City Club in San Jose—and won.

He changed his name to Antonio, which he thought was more mysterious, appropriate for a magician—but he dedicated plenty of time to learning poker as well. When he won $2,000 in a home poker game, he decided it was time to get serious. He took $900 from his winnings to the Garden City Club. Within three months, he turned that original $900 into $20,000. Antonio packed his bags and headed to Las Vegas. He was twenty-one years old, and his destination was the 1999 WSOP.

POKER AND THE MUSLIM WORLD

The Islamic faith forbids poker and other gambling games. According to the Qur'an, games of chance allow people to gain wealth without doing anything to earn it. The Prophet Muhammad forbade backgammon, chess, the rolling of dice, and all types of games in which the element of chance and easy gain is present, and conservative modern-day Muslims extend this prohibition to poker as well. According to Imam Rabbil 'Alamin,

"A person in the clutches of gambling surely has no desire to roll up his sleeves, don his overalls, and get to work. Gambling enslaves one who then becomes a mute slave in the hands of gambling and seldom succeeds in abandoning it. He thinks there is no need for working since he will eventually win, and win 'big time' one day. The Holy Prophet Muhammad said: 'To earn an honest livelihood is a duty ranking only next to the chief duty (of offering prayers).' Islam seeks to address poverty by means of hard work, and not by luck or chance. In this light, gambling only . . . makes people dependent on some sluggish whimsical impact of winning. Even if he happens to win, his greed for more increases. After having lost all his earnings, this still does not deter him from stopping, but he will gamble more in the vain hope of recovering his losses."

Ironically, however, playing cards first came to Europe from Islam, probably via Muslim Spain. These Islamic cards had four suits—cups, swords, coins, and polo sticks (seen by Europeans as clubs)—and courts consisting of a king and two male underlings. These cards crossed the Gibraltar and first appeared in Spain in 1371. Ten years later, they were everywhere in Europe.

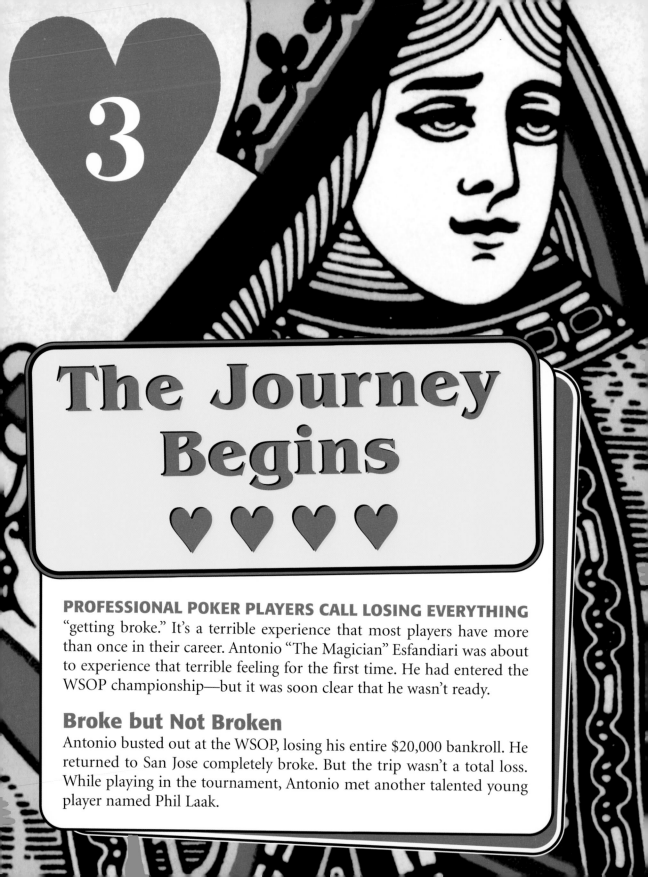

3

The Journey Begins
♥ ♥ ♥ ♥

PROFESSIONAL POKER PLAYERS CALL LOSING EVERYTHING "getting broke." It's a terrible experience that most players have more than once in their career. Antonio "The Magician" Esfandiari was about to experience that terrible feeling for the first time. He had entered the WSOP championship—but it was soon clear that he wasn't ready.

Broke but Not Broken
Antonio busted out at the WSOP, losing his entire $20,000 bankroll. He returned to San Jose completely broke. But the trip wasn't a total loss. While playing in the tournament, Antonio met another talented young player named Phil Laak.

Professional poker success was not a "given" for Antonio. There were ups and downs, especially during his early days. One of the ups for Antonio was becoming friends with other young poker players. Fellow poker player Phil "The Unabomber" Laak, shown here wearing his signature hoodie, became one of Antonio's best friends. Phil taught Antonio about poker—and about life.

Phil was also just starting his poker career. He didn't have great success at the WSOP either, but he had valuable advice for Antonio. Not only did Phil have some poker tips to share, he had some real-world advice that Antonio sorely needed, including how to keep his sense of perspective. According to PokerStars.com, Phil's philosophy on poker could be summarized this way:

"There is something to learn all the time. Sometimes it may come in the form of what NOT to do . . . but I am always trying to develop my skills. When the session is over, or even between hands, I allow

myself (sometimes liberally) the pleasure (but rarely the pain) of wins and loses. It is hard for me to see anything in poker as bad beats. Christopher Reeve falling off his horse and ending up paralyzed—that is a bad beat. Runner runner flush is not a bad beat. That is just poker.**"**

Antonio also learned other valuable lessons from his friend. Although Antonio had been supporting himself since he was seventeen, he still had no idea how to manage money. He would work for days at the restaurant, and then blow all his earnings on one night out with friends. He would win a couple thousand in a poker game, and then spend half the winnings on an expensive piece of furniture. He would build a bankroll, and then blow the whole thing in a tournament he wasn't ready to play.

With Phil's friendship and guidance, Antonio went back to San Jose to rebuild his bankroll, **refine** his game, and improve his money management both in poker and his life. Phil's guidance clearly had an effect on Antonio, because today, when people ask him about money management, he says:

"Try this with your profits: one-third to the bankroll, one-third to the party, one-third to the future. Don't forget that one-third to the future! There's no point in earning all this money if you don't have something to show for it when you're done."

The Dream Team

Eventually Antonio convinced Phil to move out to San Jose. The room-mates spent nearly all their time playing and analyzing poker. In an article by Phil Hevener for *Poker Player Newspaper*, Antonio described how the dream-team came to be:

"[Phil] came out for a weekend and just never went back home and we became very good friends and have been running around together

for the last five or six years. In a way, I guess we did come up [the ranks] together, but not from the very beginning. **"**

It was a great match-up that benefited both players immensely. From that point on, they played together, studied together, and even roomed together when traveling to tournaments. Years later, they would both reach the top and eventually move out on their own. Nevertheless, they would remain close friends, poker buddies, and business partners. In the same *Poker Player* article, Antonio explained:

Going broke is never good, but when you're a poker player, it can end a career. For players like Antonio, it's a risk that they deal with every time they sit down to play. For Antonio, losing $20,000 became almost a good thing. He learned how to better handle his money.

Irishman Phil Laak is a regular on televised poker tournaments, both as a player and as an expert commentator. He earned the nickname "The Unabomber" because, when he wears his hoodie and dark sunglasses, he bears an uncanny resemblance to the well-known drawing of the terrorist Ted Kaczynski, who called himself "Unabomber." Fortunately, Phil strikes terror only in fellow players.

"We're both good by ourselves, but we are ten times better when we are with each other."

Antonio also credits a number of other people with helping him transform into a competitive player. He names Rob Fulop, Eldon Elias, Scott Lundgren, and Gabe Thaler as people who helped him understand the game.

But while Phil and Antonio were mastering the game and taking San Jose by storm, significant changes were happening in the poker world. Soon those changes would bring both the young men into the limelight and help them rise to the very top of high-stakes poker.

The Old School

Before the 1970s, poker was a backroom game with a very bad image. It was illegal almost everywhere and had a reputation as a game for cowboys and outlaws. The people who played the game for a living were called rounders, and they were always on the move. They traveled

PHIL LAAK

Phil Laak is a relative newcomer to the poker world, but he is definitely someone people remember. He received his nickname—"The Unabomber"—because he always wears a hooded sweatshirt (with the hood up) when he's playing. His appearances on the World Poker Tour have made him one of the most popular players on the circuit and led to him landing the job as host of *E! Hollywood Holdem*.

Phil was born in Dublin, Ireland, in 1972. He became interested in tournament poker in the 1990s because of the competition, test of patience, and the many strategies that come into play during the different phases of tournaments. He believes that what helps him play poker so well is that he never allows himself to become too involved in the game's outcome, win or lose. He told PokerStars.com, "Playing well is what drives me. Not winning."

Besides being a poker player, Phil is a part-time stock market speculator and a real estate investor. He received his bachelor of science degree in mechanical engineering. One of Phil's mottos for life is, "Living well is all about optimizing, and achieving a balance between fun, freedom and fulfillment."

Young players like Antonio, Phil Laak, Jennifer Harman, and Annie Duke have poker veterans such as Doyle "Texas Dolly" Brunson to thank for the state of the game today. Poker pioneers established the WSOP, and poker popularity rolled on from there. And fortunately, many of these polished pros—including Doyle—are still around to enjoy the fruits of their efforts.

from town to town looking for action and avoiding the police who would arrest them, the cheats who would con them, and the hijackers who would rob them of their winnings.

In his famous book *Super System*, Doyle "Texas Dolly" Brunson, a legendary player who cut his teeth as a rounder, describes what poker was like in that bygone era. In Texas, one of the best places to find a poker game was Fort Worth's Exchange Street. Doyle says:

> **"I'd be surprised if you could find a tougher street in the whole world. There were shootings, muggings, robberies, and just about every kind of violence imaginable. The stuff we see on TV today is tame compared to what Exchange Street was like almost any hour of the day."**

By 1970, Doyle Brunson and other top poker players were trying to change the game's image and attract new people to the table. The WSOP, and the other tournaments it inspired, did much to attract players and improve poker's reputation. Doyle Brunson's book, *Super System*, and the many books that followed, enhanced people's knowledge of the game. In the early 1970s, World Series events were also televised for the first time.

The New School

In the late eighties through the nineties, the developing Internet began playing a role in poker's **evolution**. By the beginning of the twenty-first century, scores of people were playing poker online, mastering the computer version of the game, and then trying their hands at live-action tournaments. But despite the game's increased popularity, it still wasn't a success on television.

That was about to change. Television producer Steven Lipscomb wanted to turn poker into a popular television sport, and he thought he knew how. He was starting the WPT, a series of fully televised poker tournaments he hoped would rival the WSOP. Televised poker wasn't new, but it had never been particularly popular before. Lipscomb was sure he had the device to change everything. It was called the "hole cam."

The hole cam was introduced in Europe in 1997, but it had yet to **debut** in North America. A tiny camera mounted on the table in front of each player, the hole cam allowed viewers to see the cards the players held. Before the hole cam, television viewers could only guess at players' cards and strategies. For many viewers, especially those who didn't play poker, it made for dull television.

The World Poker Tour

With the hole cam, people watching on television have a privileged, inside view of the game that none of the players have. The viewer knows which players are holding strong cards and which are holding weak hands. People watching at home know when a player is bluffing. Because the viewers can see all the cards on the table, they also know what will happen as a result of a player's moves before the players themselves know. All these things allow viewers to see the player's strategy take shape and feel connected to the game. It makes for very exciting television.

In an interview with Russ Scott, famous professional poker player Chris Ferguson commented on how the hole cam changed televised poker:

> **"You can ask the top 100 players, this is something we don't argue about.... The innovation that created the poker explosion in my opinion, and I think in the opinion of all the top players, is the hole-card camera. The fact that you're watching incredible professionals make incredibly intelligent decisions in real time—and you know that outcome of these decisions, you know what they should choose— makes it incredibly fun."**

The first WPT tournament was played in 2002, and the first television broadcasts aired in 2003. Chris Ferguson was right: the hole cam changed everything about poker on television, and suddenly people were tuning on their sets to watch the table game in droves. And they were getting their first glimpse of a new face in the poker world.

Antonio "The Magician" Esfandiari had been working hard at his game, and he was ready for his debut in the WPT.

When the World Poker Tour came to television, viewers had an opportunity previously unavailable—they could see the players' pocket (or hole) cards. What had been a boring sport on television became exciting, with the home viewer having the best seat in the house. In this photo, Antonio (left) and Phil (hoodie) are seen playing at a WPT game.

The Magician Gets Noticed

On November 10, 2002, Antonio had his best finish to that date in a poker tournament. It happened at the WPT Gold Rush Bonanza in San Francisco. Antonio was playing in the main event, and although Paul Darden won the event and Chris Bigler grabbed second, Antonio had an impressive third-place finish. He earned $44,000 and had the additional satisfaction of beating former WSOP world champion Phil Hellmuth Jr., who came in fourth.

Antonio's Gold Rush finish was a big confidence booster, but the WPT was taking notice of him for another reason. Antonio had been

Something else happened when the WPT hit television screens. Antonio got noticed, too. His skills and style brought him fans of course, but they also caught the eye of advertisers. Antonio soon became a "face of the WPT" in commercials for the tour. The ads also gave him a chance to show off his magic skills.

virtually unknown in the poker world, but advertisers realized his skills as a magician would look great on TV. Now, he was making commercials for the WPT, featuring impressive sleight of hand with a deck of cards.

The first broadcasts of the WPT, which hit airwaves in 2003, earned impressive ratings, spurred a sudden interest in poker, and introduced Antonio Esfandiari to the world. The flashy, attractive, young magician was developing a fan base before he even won a tournament. The WPT's creator, Steven Lipscomb, told *All In*'s Lessley Anderson why Esfandiari was great for the WPT:

> **"Antonio is a young, sexy-looking magician. He's the guy who will grandstand and play it for all it's worth. And in the new world of poker, that gives him an edge. . . . He's great to watch, win or not win."**

The New Antonio

In 2003, as the WPT tournaments aired and poker's popular evolution continued, Antonio once again tried his hand at the WSOP. This time he finished in the money by placing fifth in the $2000 No Limit Hold'em event, earning $34,060. Less than a week later, he was playing in the WPT Bad Boys of Poker tournament—an invitation-only tournament featuring Gus Hansen, Paul Darden, Mark Richards, Dave Ulliot, and Antonio's close friend Phil Laak.

Antonio only finished fifth in the tournament, which Gus Hansen won. Nevertheless, the televised tournament was more great exposure for the young magician. But the rest of 2003 passed without any big tournament wins, and Antonio felt like he still hadn't really earned the popularity and fans he had gained over the course of the year.

That big win finally came in February 2004, when Antonio beat Vinnie Vinh to win the WPT L.A. Poker Classic championship and take home the nearly $1.4 million prize. Just over two months later, on May 10, 2004, Antonio won his first WSOP bracelet in $2000 Pot Limit Hold'em, earning an additional $184,860. Antonio finally had what he wanted: money, fame, and respect.

But there was still one thing to do: tell his father.

4♣

Making Magic at the Table

♣ ♣ ♣ ♣

ANTONIO'S FATHER HADN'T LIKED THE IDEA OF HIS SON
being a magician. He liked the idea of his son being a professional
gambler even less. He wished his son had a respectable profession,
like being a lawyer or a doctor. Deep down, however, he knew that
was never going to happen.

Father and Son

In an article by Aaron Todd for *Casino City Times*, Antonio recalls the
expectations his father had for him, and how his family reacted to his
decision to gamble for a living:

Being a professional poker player might not be every parent's idea of the perfect career choice for their son or daughter. It certainly wasn't what Antonio's father had in mind for his son. But there could be no arguing that Antonio worked magic when he played, and his father couldn't hide his pride in Antonio's success.

"It wasn't pretty. I come from a Persian family. If you don't plan on going to college and then Med School or to get your Master's or Ph.D., then you're not really respected in the Persian community. It's very success-oriented. So when I started gambling, [my family wasn't] too happy about it.**"**

Once Antonio's father accepted his son's career choice—and Antonio told him about his first million-dollar win—a big load was off the young poker player's shoulders. Most sons and daughters want their parents' approval, and Antonio was no exception. Now Antonio could really enjoy his life playing professional poker.

Antonio had been working for years to change his father's mind about his profession. He wanted his father to accept his choice to play poker. Even more than that, he wanted his father to truly understand and support that choice. But most of all, he wanted his father to be proud of him.

Even before Antonio's major tournament wins, his father had started to come around. The transformation in their relationship began when Antonio, determined to change his father's mind, invited him to a casino. Antonio took his father to the poker tables, and they stood together at the rails, watching the games unfold. Antonio, studying the decisions each player made, was able to tell his father what cards each player held in the pocket . . . even though there was no way to see the cards. When the cards were turned over, Antonio was correct almost every time. To his father, it must have seemed like magic, but it wasn't; he was watching a very gifted player in action. In Aaron Todd's article for *Casino City Times*, Antonio remembered what happened next:

> **"[My father] said he was proud of me, and that was about a year before I won [the L.A. Poker Classic]. He was accepting of me playing poker well before I won any tournament or got in the spotlight."**

Despite his father's acceptance, Antonio didn't tell him about the big win right away. He wanted everything to be perfect and was waiting for the right moment—so he decided to wait until the WPT Bay 101 Shooting Star tournament, which would be held in his hometown of San Jose. Antonio asked his father if he would come see him play, and Antonio's father agreed. Allyn Jaffrey Shulman's article for *Card Player* magazine describes how it happened:

> **"Many of us knew that [Antonio's] win was secret, because he wanted to tell his dad in person. He was taking his dad to the Bay 101 tournament, and before they entered the casino, he said, 'By the way, Dad, I won over a million.' Before he had time to explain, they had entered Bay 101, where Antonio**

was mobbed by friends and strangers who clamored to congratulate him. "

If Antonio's father had any remaining doubts about his son's profession, they were erased that day. Now he could truly see that Antonio was following his dream and making a very good living doing it. In an interview, Antonio's father said, "Now I tell people, 'Yes, it's his profession. My son's a poker player.'"

Becoming a Classy Player

Antonio was a champion and had his father's support, but he still had a lot of growing up to do before he could stand shoulder to shoulder with poker's greatest players. A lot of people still thought Antonio was an arrogant, obnoxious kid. His magic tricks and **antics** made him popular on television, but they didn't earn him respect among the greats in the game.

One of the players Antonio respects most is the legendary Poker Hall of Famer T. J. Cloutier. Born in 1939, T. J. is a former professional football player who has been playing high-stakes poker for decades. He holds six WSOP bracelets and has finished second in the World Series championship twice. In the world of high-stakes poker, T. J. is a legend and one of the most respected players in the field.

Antonio looked up to T. J. as a type of **mentor**. That's why it made an impact when, after Antonio gloated over a pot he won from the famous Phil Ivey, T. J. finally approached Antonio and told him in no uncertain terms that his behavior was shameful. It was time to wise up and show the other players some respect.

Now Antonio wishes he could forget some of the more embarrassing displays of his early poker days. He still always wants to be fun and entertaining at the poker table, but he tries to balance entertaining the fans with respecting the other players. An example of his progress in becoming a classy player was related by one of his friends in an article for *Bluff* magazine, who recalled being quite impressed when he saw Antonio sit down for an interview just moments after getting busted out of a televised poker match:

"Antonio handled the onscreen interview with the confidence of a seasoned TV news anchor. He was

polite, he spoke slowly with positive energy, never once stammering or blaming anybody but himself. This is not easy to do moments after one is knocked out of a poker tournament. **"**

Of course, being polite and well-mannered isn't necessarily always the best way to play a hand of poker. Sometimes getting under an opponent's skin is a **strategic** maneuver in a psychological game, so

Former professional football player T. J. Cloutier (shown on the right in this photo, along with fellow poker player Daniel Negreanu) has made a name for himself as one of the best poker players in the world. He is the proud holder of six WSOP bracelets! And he's one of the most respected players around.

fans will never see Antonio give up all his characteristic taunts and jibes. From his start in magic until now, he's always been an entertainer. In an article for lifesabluff.com he explained that he still sees himself as 80 percent entertainer and 20 percent poker player. It's just the way Antonio is.

Poker Madness

Antonio hasn't won any major tournaments since his 2004 WPT and WSOP wins, but he's still made plenty of final tables and earned a respectable amount of prize money. And fans have ample opportunity to see Antonio play on TV. In response to the WPT's success, an explosion of poker programs has hit the airwaves.

Today the Travel Channel broadcasts the WPT and the Professional Poker Tour. WSOP events and a program called *Pro-Am Poker Equalizer* are featured on ESPN. Bravo hosts *Celebrity Poker Showdown*, Fox Sports Net hosts the *Poker Superstars Invitational Tournament* and *Poker Dome Challenge*, NBC airs the *National Heads-Up Poker Championship* and *Poker After Dark*, and GSN has *Poker Royale* and *High Stakes Poker*. Poker experts and professional players like Mike Sexton, Phil Hellmuth Jr., Howard Lederer, and Robert Williamson III act as commentators for popular poker shows.

Antonio has appeared on many of these television series. In 2004, fans saw him at the table of the WPT Invitational tournament, a tournament his closest friend, Phil Laak, won, which also featured Humberto Brenes, John Juanda, Joe Cassidy, and Harry Demetriou. In the 2005/06 television season, Antonio appeared in the WPT Battle of Champions II, which was won by David Benyamine. Antonio was also in the second season of *Poker Superstars*, although he finished last. The biggest winners of that season were Johnny Chan and Todd Brunson.

In the third season of the *Poker Superstars Invitational Tournament*, Antonio redeemed himself by placing first in quarter-final and semi-final events before coming in second to Todd Brunson in the grand final and second to Mike Matusow in the championship. He also appeared in the first two seasons of *High Stakes Poker*, and appeared in the third season with Daniel Negreanu, Phil Ivey, and other famous players.

Poker fans have had the chance to watch Antonio work his magic at many televised final tables. As poker's popularity on television has grown, Antonio has appeared on many of the most popular poker programs, from NBC to Fox, to the home of televised sports—ESPN. As his exposure has grown, so has his fame.

Hollywood also likes the drama of a high-stakes poker game, and a number of movies have been made featuring real and fictional professional poker players. Some of the movies include *Rounders* with Matt Damon and Ed Norton, *Luckytown* with Kirsten Dunst, *High Roller: The Stu Ungar Story* with Michael Imperioli, and most recently *Lucky You* with Eric Bana, Drew Barrymore, and Robert Duvall. Antonio and other top pros—including Doyle Brunson, Johnny Chan, Chris Ferguson,

Jennifer Harman, Phil Hellmuth, and Daniel Negreanu—make appearances in the final film.

Wisdom from the Magician

In addition to his television appearances, Antonio has written a book called *In the Money* and signed a deal to play poker on an Internet site called Ultimate Bet. He also uses his online **forum** to give advice and

Antonio is now part of the Internet poker craze. Poker fans can ask Antonio for poker advice on the Ultimate Bet Web site. Other members of Team Ultimate Bet are shown in this photograph. Front, left to right: Jack McClelland, Annie Duke, Russ Hamilton; back, left to right: Jim Worth, Dave Ulliott, Phil Hellmuth, and Antonio.

For most people, gambling is just a game, something they do for fun. For part of the population, however, games like poker can take over their lives. Gambling becomes more than just a part of their lives—it becomes the driving force in their lives. For them, gambling is no longer fun—it's an addiction.

unreasonable chances in pursuit of food. Those who continuously gambled and won lived to have children, and thus passed along the genetic tendency to take risks. According to Dr. Pelusi:

"The possibility that a big score could be just around the corner, but you never know where or when you'll hit on it, parallels modern gambling:

> One more rock overturned and you find dinner. . . . For our ancestors, it was actually risky to avoid risk altogether. Sometimes the next big score really *is* just around the corner. If you find an edible critter behind one in 50 rocks, your foraging pays off, especially when the terrain is safe. "

Human beings seek excitement, adventure, thrills. For many of us—those of us who are fortunate enough to not live in nation not torn apart by war or famine—life is stable, predictable, safe . . . and boring. So we manufacture excitement. We play sports. We go on amusement park rides. We play poker!

Other theorists, however, find a very different answer to the question: Why do human beings play poker? According to some, people play poker not because their ordinary lives are boring but just the opposite: because their personal lives are *too* unpredictable—and poker gives them a way to control the uncertainty. For example, some psychologists might **hypothesize** that Antonio Esfandiari turned to poker because his childhood had left him feeling as though life held too many variables he could not control. Annabel Davis-Goff, author of *The Literary Companion to Gambling*, summarizes this perspective:

> "When a gambler picks up a pack of cards or a pair of dice, he feels as though he has reduced an unmanageable world to a finite, visible and comprehensive size. "

Antonio, however, probably doesn't care what his deep dark motivations are for playing poker. That's because Antonio is too busy having a good time in life.

Rocks and Rings

Lately, taping for *I Bet You* has been taking up most of Antonio's free time, even causing him to miss some recent poker tournaments. When he does have free time, he usually spends it doing the other thing he loves—partying with his friends.

Antonio is almost as famous for partying as he is for playing poker. He has tried to make having a good time into an art form, and he's gotten some of his closest friends on board. They call their

WHEN GAMBLING BECOMES UNHEALTHY

Although many people like to gamble occasionally—and there's nothing wrong with that—gambling can also become a disease. Psychologists call this "pathological gambling." An individual with this problem usually progresses from occasional gambling to habitual gambling. As the gambling progresses, the gambler begins to risk more, both personally and financially. This can lead to serious personal problems, financial ruin, and criminal behavior to support the gambling habit.

According to a December 2006 article in *Psychology Today*, the most common symptoms of pathological gambling are:

- Occasional gambling becomes habitual.

- The individual has no control over the time spent gambling.

- Gambling continues, whether winning or losing, until all money is lost or the game is terminated.

- Gambling continues until large debts are accumulated.

- The individual has a lack of concern for society's expectations and laws.

- Unlawful behavior may occur to support the habit and pay debts.

Gambling is a common behavior that is not considered a psychological disorder until the symptoms listed above are exhibited. This disorder shows similarities to substance dependence disorders and has similar symptoms. For example, many gamblers report feeling "high" because of their success; this leads to increased gambling, which in turn might result in more success, leading to overconfidence and risk-taking behavior.

Gambling addiction is a significant problem in the United States, impacting adults of all ages and their families. It affects 1 to 3 percent of all adults, men more often than women. Compulsive gambling is a chronic condition. In other words, it is an ongoing condition that does not go away without treatment—and relapse after treatment is a real risk.

So why does Antonio *really* play poker? No one—probably not even Antonio—can say for sure, but it might be because of events in his earliest childhood, or it might be because he was rebelling against his father, or maybe simply because he's good at it. Regardless of the reasons why, there are many fans just glad that he does.

group Rocks and Rings, and the group's sole purpose is to have a good fun. They take pride in wearing the best clothes, going to the most exclusive nightclubs, and always ordering the best an establishment has to offer.

Some of the rules of Rocks and Rings are that members must always wear suits when the group goes out, they always gamble to decide who pays the check, and they don't let anything get in the way of having a good time. But although they are the envy of some, Antonio and his friends have gotten some heat for their Rocks and Rings group.

Some people feel Antonio places too much emphasis on money, partying, and fame. They criticize Antonio and his Rocks and Rings **posse** for being self-centered, **elitist**, and shallow.

But the people who know him well, while admitting that Antonio can sometimes rub people the wrong way, say that the real Antonio is someone a person just can't help but like. In a *Bluff* magazine article, a friend of Antonio's described the magician:

> **"one part Aladdin, on part Bugs Bunny, Antonio is a likeable, but somewhat annoying, tall, dark, and handsome Persian wise-guy. He has a natural ability to make anybody and everybody feel like his best friend in the world. Even though you know he's feeding you a crock . . . , you just don't care. That's how charming he is. He's slick, somewhat cocky, yet at the same time, undeniably likable."**

Antonio feels that anyone who criticizes him and his lifestyle simply doesn't know who he really is. He would say his partying is based on a belief that life is short, one never knows what will happen, and it's better to enjoy success while you have it because it just might slip away.

Immigrant Gamblers

Some **sociologists** have pointed out that many immigrants are also successful gamblers. They wonder if there's a connection. Do the same characteristics that give an individual the courage to pick up his life and build a home in a totally new land also contribute to making that individual a good gambler?

In Antonio's case, it's easy to see that his early life taught him that life is filled with uncertainty. Imagine suddenly facing poverty in a land where no one understood you, and people your own age made fun of you. Imagine being nine years old and having your mother disappear—

POKER AND TEENAGERS

Initially, Antonio's father wasn't thrilled about his son's poker playing. Many parents today share Mr. Esfandiari's concern. As poker becomes a more and more popular activity for young adults, some parents worry that this trend will ultimately prove to be a destructive one.

These concerns aren't unfounded. Research indicates that when kids begin gambling before the age of eighteen, they are far more likely as adults to have unhealthy habits related to gambling. They may become gambling addicts; in other words, they might continue to gamble despite negative consequences. Poker and gambling may also expose young adults to alcohol and drug abuse.

There's another perspective on this question, however, and this one is also supported by research. Young adults who play poker have the opportunity to develop important mental skills that have to do with statistics, mathematics, and risks. Poker also helps adolescents improve their social interaction abilities by teaching them how to read expressions and gestures, as well as helping them develop self-control.

Ultimately, young adults must decide for themselves whether poker and other forms of gambling are right for them. Certain steps can help them make this decision:

- Determine if the situation (in this case, playing poker) could be damaging to themselves, to others, or to the community.

- Identify the relevant facts.

- Recognize what the options are.

- Decide which option will produce the most good and do the least harm.

- Considering all these perspectives, make a decision.

- Implement the decision.

Responsible people then reevaluate their decisions. They check to make sure things are working out as they expected. They continue to gather information and monitor their options.

On the poker circuit, Antonio is known for much more than playing poker. He loves to have a good time, and he brings his friends—the Rocks and Rings group—along with him. Antonio makes sure that everyone has a good time, friends and fans, including those fans who have fans of their own, such as Camryn Mannheim shown here (middle)!

and then never seeing her again! Life, like poker, deals out its losing hands—and you can never predict when they're coming.

At the same time, however, life in America offers immigrants a chance for prosperity. Like the poker table, American life is a fairly level playing field: pretty much everyone has the same chances for success, no matter what their social position. A royal flush may be waiting in the next hand you play.

Antonio's come a long way from the small child from Iran who landed in the United States without knowing one word of English. Antonio is enjoying his life, and he is grateful for what he has accomplished. But the young poker player isn't going to settle for what he has. He wants more, inside and beyond the game of poker.

All of this contributes to a feeling of fatalism—the belief that future events are already fixed in place and that human beings have no power to change those events. People who look at life from this perspective simply go with the flow; they believe that human initiative, willpower, and talent have little to do with life's outcomes. And so, like Antonio, they often take advantage of whatever good times come, because they never know how long they will last or when more will follow.

Antonio's Dreams

But despite Antonio's fatalistic outlook, he does have dreams. He has said that although he likes to party and have a great time with his friends, deep down what he really wants is to one day have a wife and family.

Back in his pre-poker life, Antonio considered going to culinary school, and he still thinks that one day, when he settles down and has his family, he might like to open his own restaurant. But those are still vague and faraway dreams for Antonio.

In the meantime, he continues to believe it's important to enjoy the present because no one knows what will happen in the future. In an interview for *Bluff* magazine, Antonio offered these words to live by:

> **"Life is sweet and I can't stress how important it is to live every day to its fullest. Enjoy everything you do, every place you go and everyone you meet because that's the secret—that's what happiness is all about."**

CHRONOLOGY

1970 The first World Series of Poker (WSOP) is played at Binion's Horseshoe casino.

1978 **December 8** Amir Esfandiari is born in Tehran, Iran.

1980 Iran-Iraq war begins.

1988 Amir's family moves to San Jose, California.

1997 The hole cam is used in Europe.

1999 Antonio meets Phil Laak at the WSOP.

2002 The hole cam comes to the United States.

2002 The World Poker Tour (WPT) begins.

2002 **November 10** Antonio places third in the WPT Gold Rush tournament.

2003 The first television broadcasts of the WPT air.

2004 **February 21** Antonio wins $1.4 million in WPT L.A. Poker Classic.

May 10 Antonio wins WSOP bracelet in $2000 Pot Limit Hold'em.

2006 Antonio's book *In the Money* is published.

2007 *I Bet You* premiers on cable television.

ACCOMPLISHMENTS & AWARDS

Major Tournaments Wins

2004   WPT L.A. Poker Classic: $10,000 No Limit Hold'em Championship

WSOP $2000 Pot Limit Hold'em

Television Appearances

2005   *Poker Superstars II*
Beyond the Felt

2006   *High Stakes Poker*
2006 National Heads-Up Poker Championship

2007   *I Bet You*

Movie Credits

2007   *Lucky You*
Deal (Release Date Unknown)

Books

2006   Esfandiari, Antonio. *World Poker Tour™: In The Money.*
New York: HarperCollins Publishers.

FURTHER READING & INTERNET RESOURCES

Books

Ackerman, Loren, and Christopher Ackerman. *Talkin' About Poker: Straight Talk for Parents and their Players.* Hackettstown, N.J.: High Powered Publishing LLC, 2006.

Web Sites

www.allinmag.com
All In

www.bluffmagazine.com
Bluff

www.cardplayer.com
Card Player.com

www.gamblersanonymous.org
Gambler's Anonymous Official Homepage

www.magicantonio.com
Antonio Esfandiari's Official Web Site

www.poker-babes.com
Poker Babes

www.pokerpages.com
Poker Pages.com

www.thehendonmob.com
The Hendon Mob

www.ultimatebet.com
Ultimate Bet.com

www.worldpokertour.com
World Poker Tour

GLOSSARY

antics—Amusing, frivolous, or eccentric behavior.

debut—Done for the first time.

egotistical—Having the characteristics of being selfish, self-absorbed, or self-centered.

elitist—Believing that certain people or things are superior to others and deserve special consideration.

evolution—Gradual development.

forum—A place to express oneself and discuss issues.

hypothesize—To offer something as or to form a tentative explanation for something.

mentor—Someone who is more experienced who offers assistance to a person who is less experienced.

posse—A group of people assembled for a common purpose.

refine—To improve something by making small changes.

sociologists—Individuals who study the origin, development, and structure of human society and the behavior of individuals and groups in society.

strategic—Done for reasons of strategy, a carefully devised plan of action.

Select Poker Terms

All-in—When you have put all of your playable money and chips into the pot during the course of a hand.

Ante—A prescribed amount posted before the start of a hand by all players.

Bet—The act of placing a wager in turn into the pot on any betting round, or the chips put into the pot.

Big blind—The largest regular blind in a game.

Blind—A required bet made before any cards are dealt.

Bluff—A bet or raise with a hand that is unlikely to beat the other players.

Board card—A community card in the center of the table, as in Hold'em or Omaha.

Button—A player who is in the designated dealer position.

Buy-in—The minimum amount of money required to enter any game.

Check—To waive the right to initiate the betting in a round.

Check-raise—To waive the right to bet until a bet has been made by an opponent, and then to increase the bet by at least an equal amount when it is your turn to act.

Community cards—The cards dealt face up in the center of the table that can be used by all players to form their best hand in the games of Hold'em and Omaha.

Cut—To divide the deck into two sections in such a manner as to change the order of the cards.

Discards(s)—In a draw game, the card(s) thrown away; the muck.

Face card—A king, queen, or jack.

Fixed limit—In limit poker, any betting structure in which the amount of the bet on each particular round is pre-set.

Flop—In Hold'em or Omaha, the three community cards that are turned simultaneously after the first round of betting.

Fold—To throw a hand away and relinquish all interest in a pot.

Heads-up play—Only two players involved in play.

Kicker—The highest unpaired card that helps determine the value of a five-card poker hand.

Loose—Playing more hands than normal.

Muck—(1) The pile of discards gathered facedown in the center of the table by the dealer; (2) To discard a hand.

Over card—A hole card that is higher than any other card on the board.

Play the board—Using all five community cards for your hand in Hold'em.

Pot-limit—The betting structure of a game in which you are allowed to bet up to the amount of the pot.

Raise—To increase the amount of a previous wager.

River—The final card dealt.

Showdown—The final act of determining the winner of the pot after all betting has been completed.

Small blind—In a game with multiple blind bets, the smallest blind.

Split pot—A pot that is divided among players, either because of a tie for the best hand or by agreement prior to the showdown.

Suited—Cards are of the same suit.

Tight—Playing fewer hands than normal.

Tight game—A game with less players than normal in fewer hands.

Turn—The fourth card dealt on the board during community card games.

SELECT POKER SLANG

All blue—A flush containing either clubs or spades.

All pink—A flush containing either diamonds or hearts.

Back door—Making a hand that the player wasn't drawing at.

Bad beat—A hand being beat by another hand that had a very low percentage of becoming a winning hand.

Cards speak—The face value of a hand in a showdown is the true value of the hand, regardless of a verbal announcement.

Drawing dead—Drawing to a hand that cannot win because someone already holds a hand that will beat what you are drawing to.

Potting out—Agreeing with another player to take money out of a pot, often to buy food, cigarettes, or drinks, or to make side bets.

Rags—Cards generally not worth playing.

Dolly Parton—A hand containing a 9 and a 5.

Rocket cards—Two aces.

Jackson 5—Jack and a five.

Pocket rockets—Two aces dealt face down.

Big slick—Ace and a king.

Ducks—Two 2s.

Paint—Any face card.

Rainbow—Three or four cards of different suits.

Nuts—The best possible hand.

TEXAS HOLD'EM HAND RANKINGS

The top ten Texas Hold'em hands in descending order of rank and the odds of seeing one when playing Texas Hold'em poker.

1 ROYAL FLUSH

A Ten-to-Ace straight, all in one suit
Odds against getting one: 30,939-to-1

6 STRAIGHT

A run of five card values, in any suits
Odds against getting one: 20.6-to-1

2 STRAIGHT FLUSH

A run of five card values, all in one suit
Odds against getting one: 3,590-to-1

7 THREE OF A KIND

Three cards of the same value
Odds against getting one: 19.7-to-1

3 FOUR OF A KIND

All four cards of the same value
Odds against getting one: 594-to-1

8 TWO PAIR

Two sets of two cards of the same value
Odds against getting one: 3.26-to-1

4 FULL HOUSE

Three of a kind, plus a pair (any suits)
Odds against getting one: 37.5-to-1

9 ONE PAIR

Two cards of the same value
Odds against getting one: 1.28-to-1

5 FLUSH

Five cards (any values) in the same suit
Odds against getting one: 32.1-to-1

10 HIGH CARD ONLY

A hand with no pairs, straight, or flush
Odds against getting one: 4.74-to-1

INDEX

ABOUT THE AUTHOR

Jackie Allyson is a professional children's writer who has written numerous books and articles for young people. She has lived in the United States, Canada, and Africa, and currently resides in Toronto, Ontario, with her husband and son. She enjoys the occasional game of poker with her friends, but unlike the pros, she never plays for money.

PICTURE CREDITS